JANE KWAN, CPA, CA

PERSONAL

FINANCE

FOR

TEENS

AVOID FINANCIAL PITFALLS AND UNLOCK SECRETS

TO MAKE MONEY, BUILD SAVINGS, AND INVEST IN

YOUR FUTURE

All inquiries should be made to: Honey Jar Publishing Inc. - janekwanbooks@ gmail.com

Cover design: Graph Webs - https://99designs.ca/profiles/3211932

Illustrator of job interview comic: Hermawan

Illustrator of squirrel comic: Jorge Siza

Editing and typesetting: Publishing Services

To Mom — who always provides her love and support;

To Dad — who now lives in spirit but always gave me guidance;

To my siblings, brothers-in-law, nieces and nephews – Linda, Peter, Donna, Alex, Cynthia, Amanda, Calvin, June, Anthony, Mark, Sam, Hayden, Oliver, Isabella, Claire, and Chloe – who help me in so many ways, and enrich my life with joy and happiness;
and
To Nicholas and Orion — who are the loves of my life, and the inspiration for this book

Contents

Introduction

Every morning I look at my phone and catch up on the latest news to find out what's happening in the world. Sometimes I wonder why I even do this, as the news is always depressing. The world economy, among other things, is in chaos. Inflation has run rampant, and the cost of living has skyrocketed. Interest rates are continuously increasing. It costs so much more for food and rent now. As a result, more people have started turning to food banks and increased their spending on their credit cards, which in turn has created very high debt levels.

Tuition increases every year. More students are graduating from postsecondary education but are unable to find a job. Many students wonder if it is worth it to go to university or college as they are extremely worried that they will be unable to pay the huge debt they have taken out to get their education. How do you even get a job with no experience? How can you make money if you can't get a job?

People are now working well past 65 as they realize they cannot afford to retire. Stress, anxiety, and depression affect many people's mental health, as they fear they may not have enough money to survive. Savings are non-existent. How can you save when you have so many bills to pay?

Even though there is a lot of doom and gloom in the news, there is *hope*. There are things you can do to make money, save, pay for tuition, avoid or control debt, and gain financial independence.

In this book, we'll talk about how you can get a job, even with no experience, or start a side hustle to make money.

Once you have the money, we'll get into how you can save this money and get your money working for you so that you don't have to work so hard. There's a really big advantage when you start saving and investing early. There are also tax advantages to saving which will also help to increase your wealth. You will be shocked at how exponentially your money can grow. You will be able to retire, relax, and enjoy yourself.

Budgeting is an easy but critical skill that needs to be learned. Without budgeting, you have no idea what's happening with your finances, and money can quickly disappear. I've seen start-up businesses raise millions of dollars from investors but didn't make a budget. As a result, the millions were eventually spent, with nothing left in their bank accounts! We will walk through the various budget examples I've laid out. Then, you will be able to prepare your own budget to manage your money effectively so that you don't get into financial trouble.

com/focus-areas/compensation-and-benefits/high-inflation-sees-more-canadi ans-living-paycheque-to-paycheque/370290

Earthday. (2023, n.d. n.d.). *Fashion for the earth*. Retrieved from Earthday: https://www.earthday.org/campaign/sustainable-fashion/?gclid= EAIaIQobChMIv53z_Za2_AIVnRPUAR1Bqg3qEAAYAiAAEgKCPPD_BwE

Equifax. (2023, n.d. n.d.). *Do you know your credit facts?* Retrieved from consumer.equifax: https://www.consumer.equifax.ca/personal/education/ credit-report/6-credit-facts-canadians-get-wrong/

Equifax. (2023, n.d. n.d.). *Getting a credit card: 4 things for young adults to know*. Retrieved from consumer.equifax: https://www.consumer.equifax.ca/personal/ education/credit-report/getting-a-credit-card-young-adults/

Equifax. (2023, n.d. n.d.). *How can I check credit scores?* Retrieved from Equifax: https://www.equifax.com/personal/education/credit/score/how-to-check-credit- score/

Farrington, R. (2022, September 30). *How Much Should You Have In A 529 Plan By Age*. Retrieved from thecollegeinvestor: https://thecollegeinvestor.com/ 16964/how-much-you-should-have-in-a-529-plan-by-age/

Farrington, R. (2022, October 27). *How To Save For College: Order Of Operations For Parents*. Retrieved from thecollegeinvestor: https://thecol legeinvestor.com/12113/how-to-save-for-college/

Farrington, R. (2022, October 8). *Subsidized vs. Unsubsidized Student Loans*. Retrieved from thecollegeinvestor: https://thecollegeinvestor.com/20485/under standing-subsidized-vs-unsubsidized-student-loans/

Farrington, R. (2023, January 10). *How Student Loans Work: Applying, Borrowing, and Paying Back*. Retrieved from thecollegeinvestor: https://thecol legeinvestor.com/21917/how-student-loans-work/

Farrington, R. (2023, January 28). *How To Pay For College: The Best Order Of Operations*. Retrieved from thecollegeinvestor: https://thecollegeinvestor.com/ 21877/pay-for-college/

Farrington, R. (2023, January 19). *How To Start Investing In High School*. Retrieved from thecollegeinvestor: https://thecollegeinvestor.com/4436/ started-investing-high-school/

Federal Reserve. (2022, November 4). *Central Bank Digital Currency (CBDC)*. Retrieved from Federalreserve.gov: https://www.federalreserve.gov/central- bank-digital-currency.htm

Fernando, J. (2023, January 18). *Inflation: What it is, how it can be controlled,*

and extreme examples. Retrieved from Investopedia: https://www.investope
dia.com/terms/i/inflation.asp

Fiverr. (2023, April 9). *Fiverr help.* Retrieved from Fiverr: https://www.fiverr.
com/support/articles/360010530058-Withdraw-your-earnings?segment=seller

Fiverr. (2023, n.d. n.d.). *Seller taxes.* Retrieved from Fiverr: https://www.fiverr.
com/support/articles/360010561178-Seller-taxes?segment=seller

Fiverr. (2023, n.d. n.d.). *W-9 collection.* Retrieved from Fiverr: https://www.fiverr.
com/support/articles/360011135837-W-9-Collection?segment=seller

Flynn, J. (2022, November 3). *25+ Amazon statistics [2023]: Facts about the
largest U.S. E-commerce market.* Retrieved from Zippia: https://www.zippia.
com/advice/amazon-statistics/

Frankenfield, J. (2022, November 22). *What is Bitcoin? How to mine, buy, and use
it.* Retrieved from Investopedia: https://www.investopedia.com/terms/b/
bitcoin.asp

Frankenfield, J. (2023, February 4). *Cryptocurrency Explained With Pros and
Cons for Investment.* Retrieved from Investopedia: https://www.investopedia.
com/terms/c/cryptocurrency.asp#toc-how-do-you-buy-cryptocurrencies

Frenette, M. (2019, January 23). *Are the Career Prospects of Postsecondary
Graduates Improving?* Retrieved from 150.statcan.gc: https://www150.stat
can.gc.ca/n1/pub/11f0019m/11f0019m2019003-eng.htm

Freshbooks. (2023, January 27). *How much money do you have to make to not file
taxes?* Retrieved from Freshbooks: https://www.freshbooks.com/hub/taxes/
how-much-money-do-you-have-to-make-to-not-pay-taxes

Ganti, A. (2022, May 28). *What Is a Brokerage Fee? How Fees Work, Types, and
Expense.* Retrieved from Investopedia: https://www.investopedia.com/terms/b/
brokerage-fee.asp

Gillespie, L. (2022, December 20). *The latest rules of tipping: How much to tip in
2023.* Retrieved from Bankrate: https://www.bankrate.com/personal-finance/
how-much-to-tip/

Government of Canada. (2021, June 17). *Paying back student debt.* Retrieved
from Canada: https://www.canada.ca/en/financial-consumer-agency/services/
pay-down-student-debt.html

Government of Canada. (2022, November 10). *Canada Education Savings Grant.*
Retrieved from Canada: https://www.canada.ca/en/revenue-agency/services/
tax/individuals/topics/registered-education-savings-plans-resps/canada-educa
tion-savings-programs-cesp/canada-education-savings-grant-cesg.html

Government of Canada. (2022, December 28). *Canada Pension Plan: Pensions and benefits monthly amounts.* Retrieved from Canada: https://www.canada. ca/en/services/benefits/publicpensions/cpp/payment-amounts.html

Government of Canada. (2022, November 2). *CPP contribution rates, maximums and exemptions.* Retrieved from Canada: https://www.canada.ca/en/revenue-agency/services/tax/businesses/topics/payroll/payroll-deductions-contribu tions/canada-pension-plan-cpp/cpp-contribution-rates-maximums-exemptions.html

Government of Canada. (2022, November 16). *EI Premium rates and maximums.* Retrieved from Canada: https://www.canada.ca/en/revenue-agency/services/ tax/businesses/topics/payroll/payroll-deductions-contributions/employment-insurance-ei/ei-premium-rates-maximums.html

Government of Canada. (2022, August 5). *Getting your credit report and credit score.* Retrieved from Canada: https://www.canada.ca/en/financial-consumer-agency/services/credit-reports-score/order-credit-report.html#toc3

Government of Canada. (2022, November 10). *How an RESP works.* Retrieved from Canada: https://www.canada.ca/en/revenue-agency/services/tax/individu als/topics/registered-education-savings-plans-resps/resp-works.html

Government of Canada. (2022, August 5). *Paying off your credit card.* Retrieved from Canada: https://www.canada.ca/en/financial-consumer-agency/services/ credit-cards/pay-off-credit-card.html

Government of Canada. (2023, January 30). *8.3.6 Non-refundable and refundable tax credits* . Retrieved from Canada: https://www.canada.ca/en/financial-consumer-agency/services/financial-toolkit/taxes/taxes-3/7.html

Government of Canada. (2023, January 16). *CPP Retirement pension.* Retrieved from Canada: https://www.canada.ca/en/services/benefits/publicpensions/ cpp.html

Government of Canada. (2023, February 4). *Old age security payment amounts.* Retrieved from Canada: https://www.canada.ca/en/services/benefits/publicpen sions/cpp/old-age-security/payments.html

Government of Canada. (2023, January 26). *Purpose of taxes.* Retrieved from Canada: https://www.canada.ca/en/revenue-agency/services/tax/individuals/ educational-programs/purpose-taxes.html#lsn-a-prt2

Hanson, M. (2022, October 24). *Average Cost of College & Tuition.* Retrieved from Educationdata: https://educationdata.org/average-cost-of-college

Hazell, A. (2022, December 9). *Compound interest calculator.* Retrieved from thecalculatorsite: https://www.thecalculatorsite.com/finance/calculators/ compoundinterestcalculator.php

Henricks, M. (2022, December 30). *Robo Advisor Fees: How Much It Costs.* Retrieved from Smartasset: https://smartasset.com/investing/robo-advisor-fees

Huddleston Jr., T. (2022, December 25). *Mark Cuban's advice for young people starting a business: "It really comes down to one simple thing".* Retrieved from CNBC: https://www.cnbc.com/2022/12/25/mark-cuban-top-advice-for-young-people-starting-a-business.html

Indeed editorial team. (2022, November 17). *19 Good jobs for teens to consider (with salaries).* Retrieved from Indeed: https://ca.indeed.com/career-advice/finding-a-job/good-jobs-for-teens

Indeed editorial team. (2022, December 4). *Interview preparation tips.* Retrieved from Indeed: https://ca.indeed.com/career-advice/interviewing/interview-preparation

Kagan, J. (2022, April 10). *Digital wallet explained: Types with examples and how it works.* Retrieved from Investopedia: https://www.investopedia.com/terms/d/digital-wallet.asp

Kagan, J. (2022, December 27). *Federal income tax.* Retrieved from Investopedia: https://www.investopedia.com/terms/f/federal_income_tax.asp

Kagan, J. (2022, November 27). *What is PayPal and how does it work?* Retrieved from Investopedia: https://www.investopedia.com/terms/p/paypal.asp

Lambarena, M. (2021, February 24). *How is credit card interest calculated?* Retrieved from Nerdwallet: https://www.nerdwallet.com/article/credit-cards/how-is-credit-card-interest-calculated

Lev, E. (2022, December 13). *A new taxi scam has hit the streets of Toronto. Here's what to look out for.* Retrieved from Yahoo: https://ca.style.yahoo.com/taxi-scam-toronto-debit-card-174455709.html

Lioudis, N. (2022, September 27). *How Does an Investor Make Money On Bonds?* Retrieved from Investopedia: https://www.investopedia.com/ask/answers/how-does-investor-make-money-on-bonds/

Mackenzie Investments. (2021, November n.d.). *Mackenzieinvestments.* Retrieved from A guide to investment fund distributions: https://www.mackenzieinvestments.com/content/dam/mackenzie/en/brochures/wp-a-guide-to-investment-fund-distributions-en.pdf

Marquit, M., & Reilly-Larke, C. (2022, August 12). *How To Buy Mutual Funds.* Retrieved from Forbes: https://www.forbes.com/advisor/ca/investing/how-to-buy-mutual-funds/

Masterson, V. (2022, September 6). *Explainer: What are meme stocks?* Retrieved from Weforum: https://www.weforum.org/agenda/2022/09/what-are-meme-stocks-explainer/

Maverick, J. (2021, April 20). *What Is a Good Expense Ratio for Mutual Funds?* Retrieved from Investopedia: https://www.investopedia.com/ask/answers/032715/when-expense-ratio-considered-high-and-when-it-considered-low.asp

Maverick, J. (2023, January 4). *Is Dividend Income Taxable?* Retrieved from Investopedia: https://www.investopedia.com/ask/answers/090415/dividend-income-taxable.asp

Michaels, J. (2023, February 1). *Side hustles for teens - 20 best ways to start making money today.* Retrieved from Frugalforless: https://www.frugalforless.com/side-hustles-for-teens/

MoneyGuide Network Inc. (2023, February 3). *Daily interest savings account rates.* Retrieved from Moneyguide: https://moneyguide.ca/daily-interest-savings-accounts/

Mydoh. (2023, January 12). *INVESTING 101: A GUIDE FOR PARENTS AND TEENAGERS .* Retrieved from Mydoh: https://www.mydoh.ca/learn/money-101/investing/investing-101-a-guide-for-parents-and-teenagers/

National Bank. (2023, n.d. n.d.). *How do I get a cash advance on my credit card?* Retrieved from NBC: https://www.nbc.ca/personal/help-centre/credit-card/transactions/credit-card-cash-advance.html

O'Brien, S. (2022, November 18). *Employers are planning pay increases of 4.6% in 2023, slightly above this year's 4.2%, study shows.* Retrieved from CNBC: https://www.cnbc.com/2022/11/18/employers-plan-2023-pay-increases-of-4point6percent-slightly-above-2022s-4point2percent.html

Okafor, J. (2022, December 8). *Negative impact of technology on the environment.* Retrieved from TRVST: https://www.trvst.world/environment/negative-impact-of-technology-on-the-environment/

Ontario Colleges. (2023, n.d. n.d.). *Paying for College: Tuition and Financial Assistance.* Retrieved from Ontariocolleges: https://www.ontariocolleges.ca/en/colleges/paying-for-college

Orem, T. (2022, October 21). *Self-employment tax: what it is and how to calculate it.* Retrieved from Nerdwallet: https://www.nerdwallet.com/article/taxes/self-employment-tax

Rate Inflation. (2023, January 17). *Canadian inflation rate.* Retrieved from Rateinflation: https://www.rateinflation.com/inflation-rate/canada-inflation-rate/

Reiff, N. (2022, April 8). *How Do Cryptocurrency Exchange-Traded Funds*

(ETFs) Work? Retrieved from Investopedia: https://www.investopedia.com/investing/understanding-cryptocurrency-etfs/

Reiff, N. (2023, January 4). *The Collapse of FTX: What Went Wrong With the Crypto Exchange?* Retrieved from Investopedia: https://www.investopedia.com/what-went-wrong-with-ftx-6828447

Rolfe, K. (2022, October 18). *What is the stock market and how does it work?* Retrieved from theglobeandmail: https://www.theglobeandmail.com/investing/article-what-is-stock-market-canada/?utm_source=Offsite&utm_medium=PaidSearch&utm_campaign=traffic_mkt&utm_term=rob&utm_content=StockMarket_Creative2&gclid=

Segal, T. (2022, April 6). *What is a central bank, and does the U.S. have one?* Retrieved from Investopedia: https://www.investopedia.com/terms/c/centralbank.asp

Settlement.org. (2019, February 13). *What is Cooperative Education for High School Students?* Retrieved from Settlement.org: https://settlement.org/ontario/education/elementary-and-secondary-school/school-systems-in-ontario/what-is-cooperative-education-for-high-school-students/

Social Security. (2015, November n.d.). *Education and Lifetime Earnings.* Retrieved from SSA: https://www.ssa.gov/policy/docs/research-summaries/education-earnings.html

Statista. (2022, October 27). *Median annual earnings of high school diploma holders in the United States from 1990 to 2021.* Retrieved from Statista: https://www.statista.com/statistics/642042/average-annual-salary-of-us-high-school-graduates/

Statistics Canada. (2022, September 9). *Chart 1 Average undergraduate tuition fees for Canadian full-time students, by province or territory, 2022/2023.* Retrieved from 150.statcan.gc: https://www150.statcan.gc.ca/n1/daily-quotidien/220907/cg-b001-png-eng.htm

Statistics Canada. (2022, September 27). *Who pays for a university education?* Retrieved from Statcan.gc: https://www.statcan.gc.ca/o1/en/plus/1896-who-pays-university-education

Talent. (2023, n.d. n.d.). *High school student average salary in Canada, 2023.* Retrieved from ca.talent: https://ca.talent.com/salary?job=high+school+student

TD. (2023, n.d. n.d.). *Gold ETFs.* Retrieved from TD: https://www.td.com/ca/en/investing/direct-investing/articles/gold-etfs

The Canadian Press. (2022, November 4). *Federal student loan interest to be permanently eliminated: fiscal update.* Retrieved from Nationalpost: https://nationalpost.com/news/politics/fiscal-update-2022-ottawa-to-permanently-eliminate-student-loan-interest

The Canadian Press Staff. (2022, September 27). *Employers in these provinces are projecting the largest average salary increases next year.* Retrieved from CTVnews: https://www.ctvnews.ca/business/employers-in-these-provinces-are-projecting-the-largest-average-salary-increases-next-year-1.6086018

The Investopedia Team. (2022, September 18). *Credit score: Definition, factors, and improving it.* Retrieved from Investopedia: https://www.investopedia.com/terms/c/credit_score.asp

The Investopedia team. (2022, February 8). *Form W-2 Wage and tax statement: What it is and how to read it.* Retrieved from Investopedia: https://www.investopedia.com/terms/w/w2form.asp

Thompson, A. (2022, August 27). *How much does it cost to rent a 1 bedroom apartment in 2022?* Retrieved from Talktomira: https://www.talktomira.com/post/how-much-does-it-cost-to-rent-a-1-bedroom-apartment-in-2022

Tsosie, C. (2022, May 9). *11 Things to know before getting your first credit card.* Retrieved from Nerdwallet: https://www.nerdwallet.com/article/credit-cards/things-to-know-first-credit-card?trk_channel=web&trk_copy

United States Government. (2023, January 4). *Understanding Employment taxes.* Retrieved from IRS: https://www.irs.gov/businesses/small-businesses-self-employed/understanding-employment-taxes

Upwork. (2023, n.d. n.d.). *Freelancer service fees.* Retrieved from Upwork: https://support.upwork.com/hc/en-us/articles/211062538-Freelancer-Service-Fees

Weyman, S. (2023, January 31). *Best ETFs In Canada 2023.* Retrieved from Moneygenius: https://moneygenius.ca/investing/etfs

Wikipedia. (2022, December 12). *Nikkei 225.* Retrieved from en.wikipedia: https://en.wikipedia.org/wiki/Nikkei_225

Wikipedia. (2022, December 21). *S&P/TSX Composite Index.* Retrieved from en.wikipedia: https://en.wikipedia.org/wiki/S%26P/TSX_Composite_Index

Wikipedia. (2022, April 28). *Time deposit.* Retrieved from en.wikipedia: https://en.wikipedia.org/wiki/Time_deposit

Wikipedia. (2023, January 31). *Dow Jones Industrial Average.* Retrieved from en.wikipedia: https://en.wikipedia.org/wiki/Dow_Jones_Industrial_Average

Woodfield, T. (2021, June 14). *TFSA vs Roth IRA - What are the differences?*

Retrieved from Swanwealthcoaching: https://www.swanwealthcoaching.com/blog/2021/06/14/tfsa-vs-roth-ira-what-are-the-differences

Yahoo Finance. (2023, January 22). *Finance.yahoo.* Retrieved from Bitcoin USD (BTC-USD): https://finance.yahoo.com/quote/BTC-USD/history/?

Yahoo Finance. (2023, January 20). *GameStop Corp. (GME).* Retrieved from finance.yahoo: https://finance.yahoo.com/quote/GME/history?

Yocket Editorial Team. (2022, December 2). *University vs College Canada: Difference Between College And University In Canada.* Retrieved from Yocket: https://yocket.com/blog/university-vs-college-in-canada